A YEAR IN PICTURES: 1985

Concept and archive development: **Ted Cockle**

Design: **Jac Harries**

Full gratitude to Christopher Sleet at Getty Images

ISBN: 978-1-3999-9207-7

M·P

MUSSEL
PUBLICATIONS

1985 OVERVIEW

This book features the most fun, fascinating and memorable images of the year 1985.

Ronald Reagan is sworn in for a second term as President and meets with Mikhail Gorbachev, the de facto leader of the Soviet Union, for the first time.

Coca-Cola changes its formula to New Coke, but the response is overwhelmingly negative, and the original formula is back on the market in less than three months.

In the UK, the best-selling cars are the Ford Escort, the Vauxhall Cavalier, and the Ford Fiesta. Garlic bread first becomes popular this year. The soap opera 'Neighbours' debuts in Australia on the Seven Network, and 'EastEnders' debuts on the BBC in the UK.

Major music artist releases this year include albums from Bruce Springsteen, Madonna, and Whitney Houston. Michael Jackson buys ATV Music for $47 million, which includes every Beatles song. The charity single 'We Are The World' is recorded to assist with famine aid and features Michael Jackson, Lionel Richie, Stevie Wonder, and Cyndi Lauper. In July, the Live Aid benefit concerts take place at Wembley Stadium in London and the John F. Kennedy Stadium in Philadelphia, instigated by Bob Geldof and Midge Ure, and they raise over £50 million for famine relief in Ethiopia.

'Back to the Future', 'Rambo: First Blood Part II', and 'Rocky IV' are the highest-grossing US movies this year. The film 'Amadeus' wins Best Picture at the Academy Awards. 'A View to a Kill' is released, which is the last James Bond film to star Roger Moore.

Please enjoy the journey through all the images that created the full experience of 1985.

CELEBRITIES BORN IN 1985

Lewis Hamilton 07/01

Doutzen Kroes 23/01

J Cole 28/01

Rag N Bone Man 29/01

Cristiano Ronaldo 05/02

Marvin Humes 18/03

Keira Knightley 26/03

Beth Twiddle 01/04

Leona Lewis 03/04

Taio Cruz 23/04

Gal Gadot 30/04

Lily Allen 02/05

Fernandinho 04/05

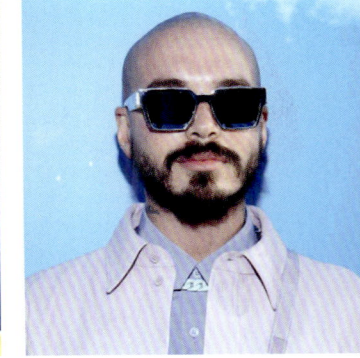

J Balvin 07/05

Chris Froome 20/05

Mutya Buena 21/05

Carey Mulligan 28/05

Charlie Simpson 07/06

Nadine Coyle 15/06

Lana Del Ray 21/06

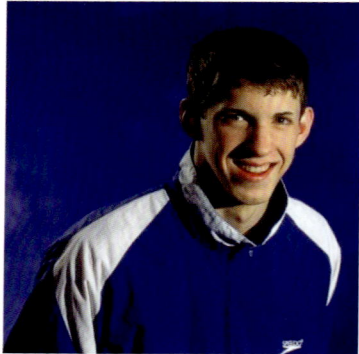

Michael Phelps 30/06

Phoebe Waller Bridge 14/07

Tom Fletcher 17/07

Anna Kendrick 19/08

Nipsey Hussle 15/08

T-Pain 03/09

Luka Modric 19/09

Nicola Roberts 05/10

Bruno Mars 08/10

Miguel 23/10

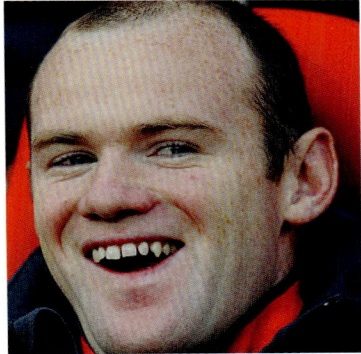

Wayne Rooney 24/10

Ciara 25/10

Lily Aldridge 15/11

Carly Rae Jepsen 21/11

Janelle Monae 01/12

Greg James 17/12

Gary Cahill 19/12

Tom Sturridge 21/12

UK LIFE

MINERS STRIKE

Between 1984 and 1985, major industrial action was undertaken within the British coal industry in an attempt to prevent colliery closures, turning into one of the most bitter industrial disputes in British history.

The campaign was led by Arthur Scargill of the National Union of Mineworkers (NUM) against the government agency, the National Coal Board (NCB). The Conservative government, led by Prime Minister Margaret Thatcher, opposed the strike and also aimed to reduce the power of the trade unions. During the year-long strike, there were many violent confrontations.

The strike came to an end on 3rd March 1985, declared illegal due to the lack of a national ballot in the previous September.

BUCKINGHAM PALACE

In July, Michael Fagan scaled the perimeter wall of Buckingham Palace and climbed a drainpipe. Fagan entered the palace and walked the corridors for several minutes before entering the bedroom of Queen Elizabeth II. The Queen departed the room to alert security and seek urgent help. Fagan was committed for psychiatric evaluation.

SINCLAIR C5

This vehicle was developed by Clive Sinclair, who had developed home computers in the early 1980s. The C5 was built to be a new breed of ambitious electric vehicle and was launched in January. Despite its big ambitions, its top speed of 15 mph, lack of weatherproofing, and limited battery range restricted its reception by the general public. Production unfortunately stopped entirely by August.

POLITICS

CONSERVATIVE PARTY

Margaret Thatcher's second term of office as Prime Minister of the UK began in 1983, and she remained in office until 1990.

Ronald Reagan was sworn in for a second term of office as President of the USA this year, and Thatcher visited him at the White House in Washington in November.

TORY GOVERNMENT

The Tory Party conference took place in October in Blackpool this year.

David Mellor Home Office Minister

Keith Joseph Secretary Of State for Education

Nigel Lawson Chancellor Of The Exchequer

Kenneth Baker Secretary of State for the Environment

Jeffrey Archer Deputy Chairman

OPPOSITION PARTIES

Neil Kinnock was the leader of the Labour Party. He confronted the extremist elements within his own party, signalling a shift to a more centrist Labour Party.

Kinnock + Tina Turner

Red Wedge movement featuring Paul Weller + Billy Bragg

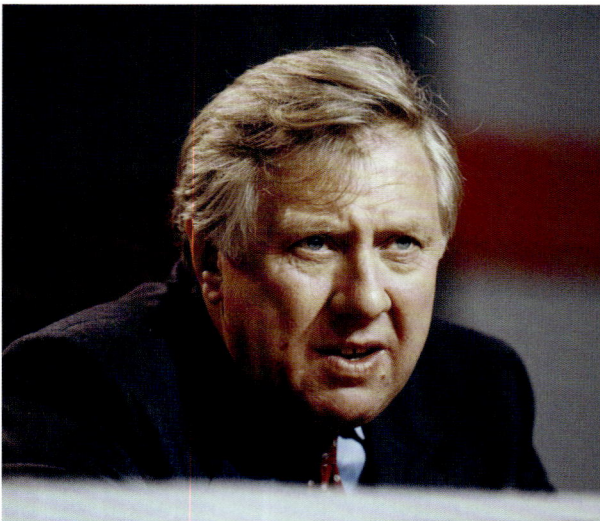

Roy Hattersley – Labour politician

SDP Politicians Roy Jenkins, David Owen and Bill Rodgers

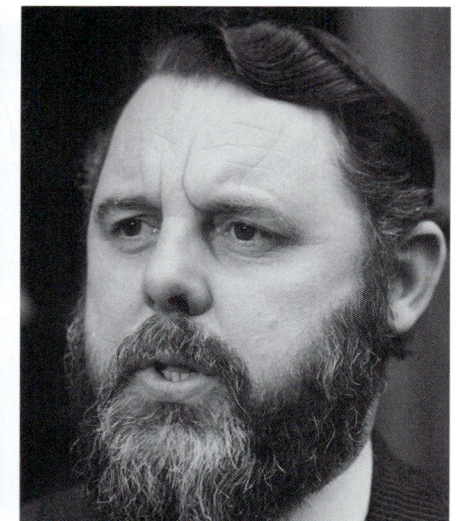

British envoy for the Church of England Terry Waite who was involved in negotiating the release of hostages in Libya.

ROYALTY

QUEEN ELIZABETH

This was her 33rd year on the throne, and events this year included visiting Portugal, attending Royal Ascot, and riding her horse Burmese at the Trooping of the Colour in June.

The Queen Mother with Lady Diana + Prince Edward

The Queen Mother with Princess Anne

LADY DIANA + PRINCE CHARLES

Prince Charles married Diana Spencer in July 1981, and their first son, William, arrived in June 1982, followed by their second son, Harry, in September 1984.

Lady Diana

Princess Anne

Prince Charles stood here with his son William and the publisher Robert Maxwell.

Lady Diana + Princess Margaret

SPORT

FOOTBALL: LUTON TOWN VS MILLWALL RIOT

A riot took place at the match between Luton Town and Millwall during the FA Cup quarter final. Seats are torn down and thrown on to the pitch, before a pitch invasion then took place. The riots continued in the streets near the stadium and 81 people were injured. Luton Town won the game 1-0.

Millwall manager George Graham speaking to police

BRADFORD FIRE

In May a fire engulfs a wooden stand at the Valley Parade in Bradford killing 56 people.

HEYSEL STADIUM DISASTER

39 spectators were killed at the European Cup final between Liverpool and Juventus (0-1) at the Heysel Stadium in Brussels, Belgium.

The Football Association chose to ban all English football clubs from playing in Europe in response to this incident. The following month, UEFA banned all English football clubs from European competitions for an indefinite period, recommending that Liverpool should serve an extra three years of exclusion once all other English clubs have been reinstated.

FIRST DIVISION

Everton became the league champions in May and later that month they lift the European Cup Winners Cup with a 3-1 win over Rapid Vienna in Rotterdam.

Their players include Gary Lineker, who was the top scorer in the league this year, alongside Chelsea's Kerry Dixon, and their captain Derek Mountfield, seen here kissing the First Division trophy after their match at Goodison Park against West Ham.

FA CUP

In June, the FA Cup final took place between Manchester United and the holders, Everton. United won by a single goal, scored in extra time by Norman Whiteside, who curled it past Neville Southall. (Kevin Moran was sent off for a foul on Peter Reid).

Here is Paul McGrath of United preparing to take on Graeme Sharp of Everton, and key United player Mark Hughes.

Chelsea this season featured talents such as Pat Nevin and lead goal scorer Kerry Dixon. Ken Bates, owner of Chelsea Football Club, shows off the new electric perimeter fence at Stamford Bridge. The fence was erected between the stands and the pitch after a number of pitch invasions by football hooligans.

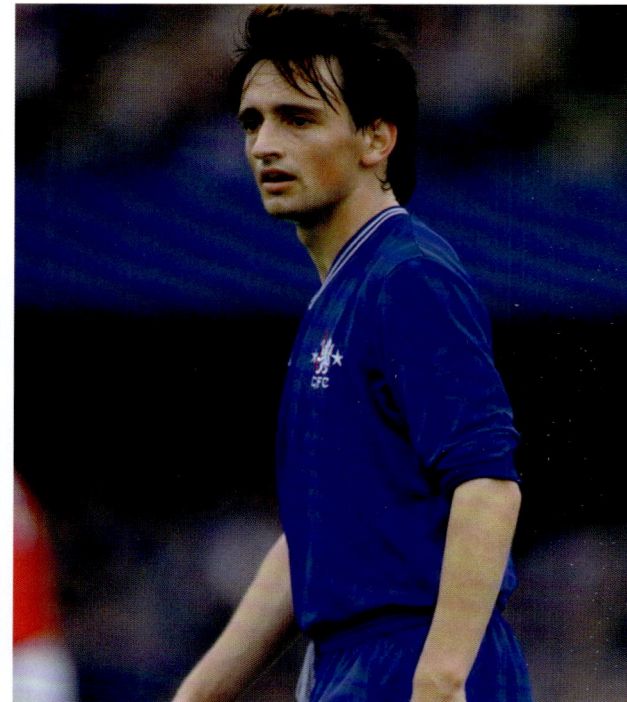

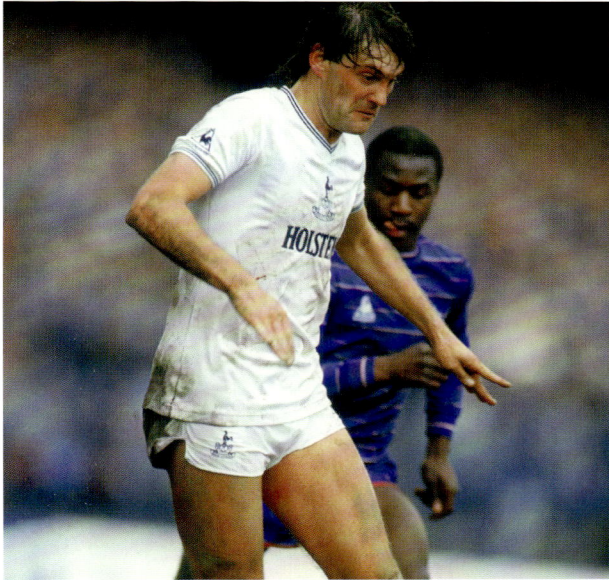
Glenn Hoddle was a key player at Tottenham.

Charlie George at Arsenal

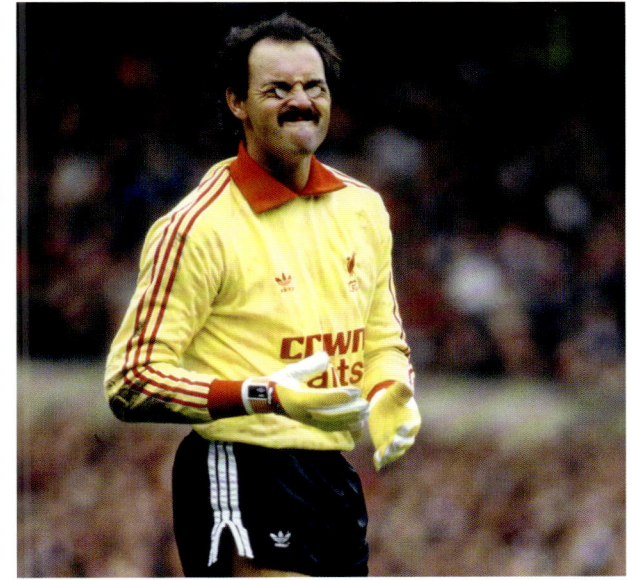
Bruce Grobbelaar at Liverpool

John Barnes at Watford

On the International arena, Diego Maradona was the star of the Argentina side.

The excellent Brazilian team this year featured such talent as Zico & Socrates.

In September, the England football team secures qualifications for the 1986 Mexico World Cup after drawing 1-1 with Romania at Wembley, with Tottenham midfielder Glenn Hoddle scoring Englands goal.

The England manager is Bobby Robson, Gary Lineker managed to score a hat trick in October at Wembley in a World Cup Qualifier against Turkey, and other key players include Ray Wilkins and Bryan Robson

TENNIS: WIMBLEDON THIS YEAR

Boris Becker beat Kevin Curren in the men's final, becoming the first unseeded player and first German to win the Wimbledon singles title, as well as being the youngest ever male major singles champion at 17. McEnroe had lost in the semifinals.

Mens doubles: Heinz Gunthardt (Swiss) + Balazs Taroczy (Hungary) beat Pat Cash (Aus) + John Fitzgerald (Aus).

Ivan Lendl

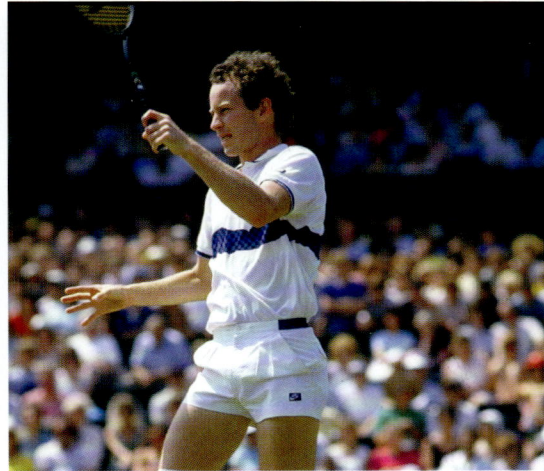

John McEnroe

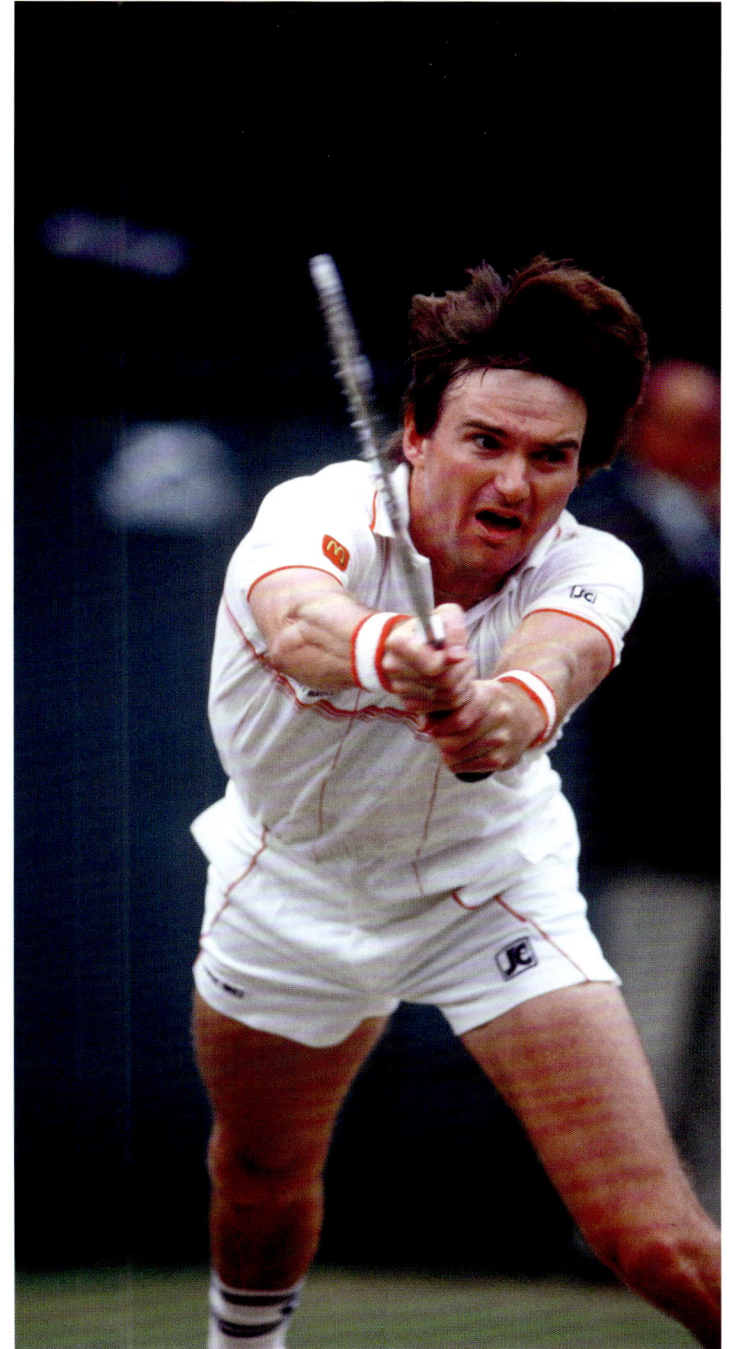

Jimmy Connors

Martina Navratilova beat Chris Evert Lloyd in the women's final, winning her 6th Wimbledon title.

Women's doubles: Kathy Jordan (US) + Elizabeth Smylie (Aus) beat Martina Navratilova (US) + Pam Shriver (US).

Chris Evert Lloyd

Steffi Graf

GOLF

USA team Captain Ray Floyd (left) and European team Captain Tony Jacklin (right) of England pose with the trophy during the Ryder Cup at The Belfry Golf Club in Sutton Coldfield, England. Europe won the event with a score of 16.5-11.5.

Sandy Lyle of Scotland alongside his wife Christine and son Stuart the day after winning the British Open at Royal St Georges Golf Club in Sandwich, Kent.

CRICKET

IAN BOTHAM

VIV RICHARDS

In February, Botham went on trial for posession of Cannabis. In October, he completed a charity walk from John O' Groats to Lands End.

Viv Richards of Somerset topped the batting averages this year. The leading run scorer was Essex and England batsman Graham Gooch. Richard Ellison of Kent and England topped the bowling averages and Neal Radford was leading wicket taker.

ENGLAND

England won the Ashes in September thanks to the batting of Mike Gatting, Tim Robinson and David Gower, and some excellent seam bowling by Richard Ellison.

England team before the fifth test at Edgbaston.

David Gower

Gatting achieved his first test century for England during the test at Madras in India.

The English team in front of the Taj Mahal.

MOTOR RACING

The British Grand Prix was won in July by Alain Prost driving a Mclaren. Michele Alboreto was second and Jacques Laffite came third.

BOXING

In April a fight called 'The War' takes place between Marvin Hagler and Tommy Hearns. The fight takes place at Caesars Palace in Las Vegas. This a world middle weight championship fight. Hagler wins the fight by a third round knockout. Many consider this to be the greatest three rounds in boxing history, with constant action, drama and violent back and forth exchanges.

Mike Tyson made his professional debut this year.

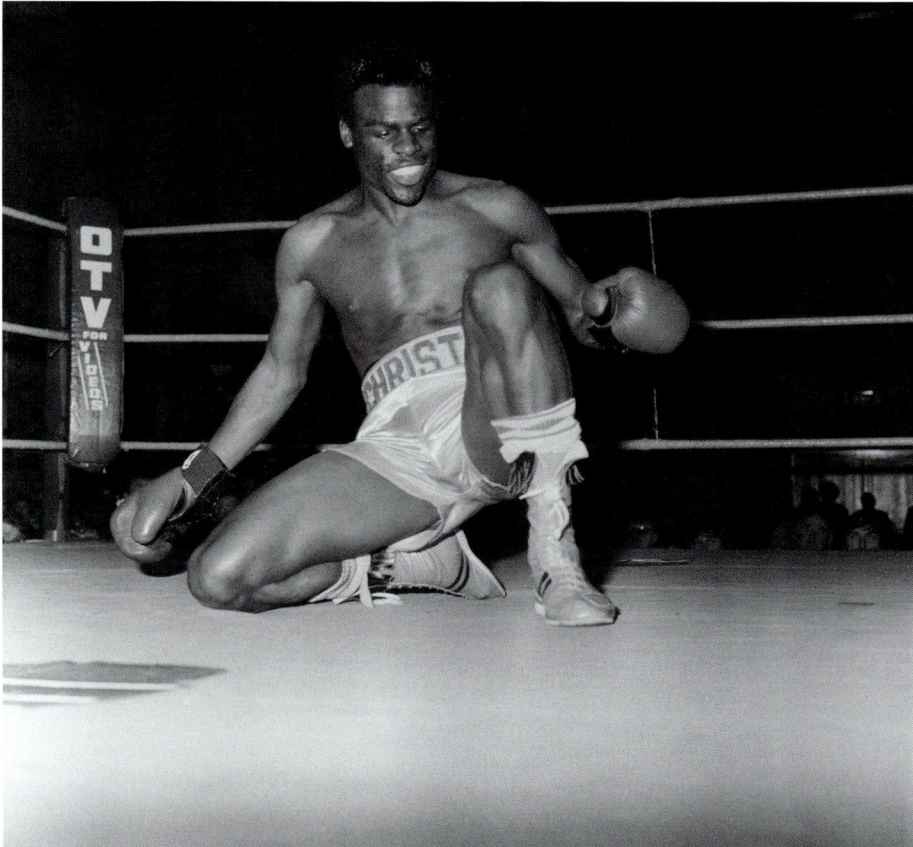

Barry McGuigan took on long-reigning WBA featherweight champion, Eusebio Pedroza of Panama for a world title fight. The fight took place at the Loftus Road football stadium in London. McGuigan became the champion by dropping Pedroza in round seven and winning a unanimous fifteen-round decision. Later that year, Barry was named BBC Sports Personality of the Year, becoming the first person not born in the United Kingdom to win the award.

Errol Christie

ATHLETICS

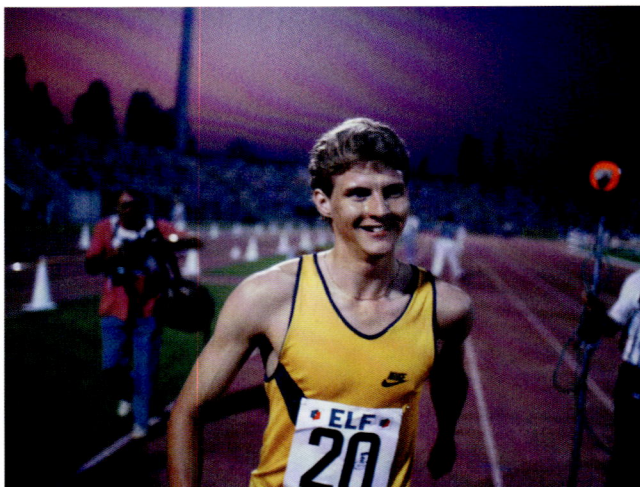

Steve Cram set a new world record time for the 1500m of 3 min 29secs in Nice, France.

Ed Moses of the US won 107 consecutive finals out of 122 consecutive races between 1977 and 1987. Here he is just after winning gold at the 1984 Olympics.

Zola Budd won the 5000m with a new world record for 14.48 minutes.

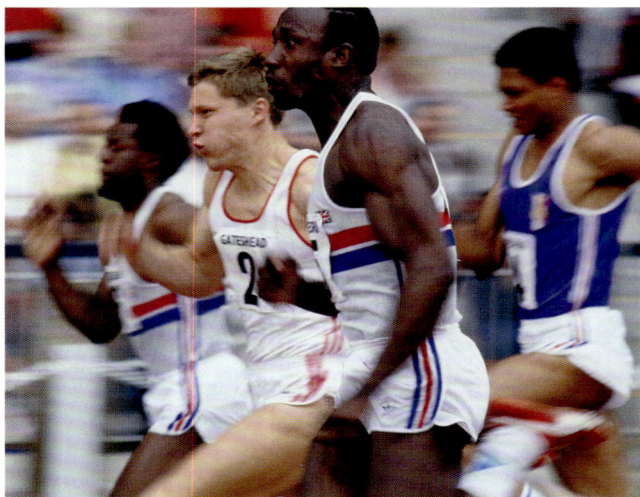

Linford Christie of Great Britain running in the Mens 100 metres at the Gateshead International Stadium.

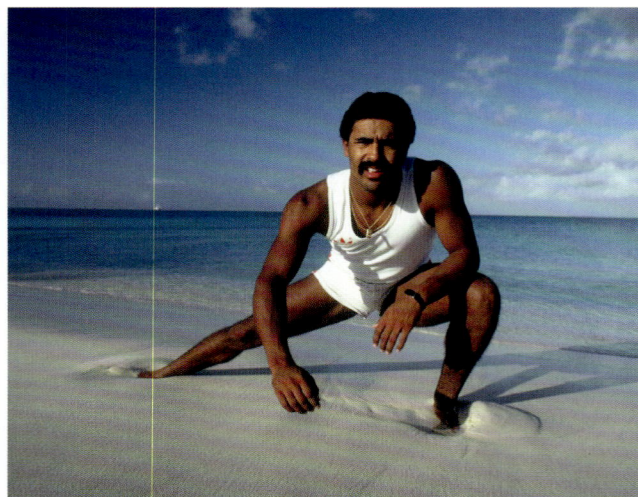

Daley Thompson. Gold medal winner in Decathlon at the Los Angeles Olympics.

DARTS

Eric Bristow entered the Embassy World Darts Championship at the Jollees Cabaret Club in Stoke On Trent as defending champion. Jocky Wilson managed to reach the quarter finals but Bristow ultimately won the title, beating John Lowe in the final.

Jocky Wilson

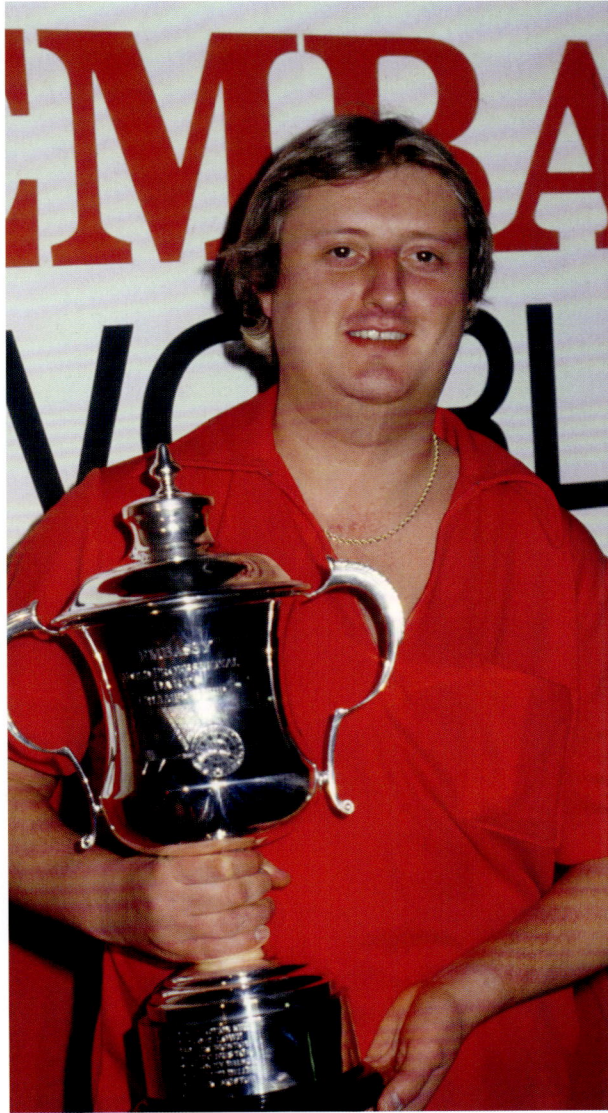

Eric Bristow

John Lowe

SNOOKER

This years Embassy World Snooker Championship was broadcast in the UK by the BBC, the winners prize was £60 000.

The final was between Dennis Taylor from Northern Ireland and the defending champion Englishman Steve Davis. The match was decided on the black ball in a deciding frame and Taylor ultimately potted the ball to win his sole World Championship. This match is widely considered to be one of the finest matches in Snooker history and prompted a major surge in the sports popularity. 18.5 million people watched this final.

Dennis Taylor

Steve Davis

Alex Hurricane Higgins

ICE SKATING

Torville & Dean remained very much in a glow of publicity following their spectacular win of the gold medal for ice dancing at the 1984 Sarajevo Winter Olympics. It was here that the duo received twelve perfect 6.0's after skating to Maurice Revel's 'Bolero'. More than 24 million people watched this making it one of the most watched television events ever in the UK.

RUGBY

Rory Underwood overlooking the scrum in the Five Nations match against Scotland at Twickenham.

Rob Andrew in the Five Nations match against France at Twickenham.

CITY LIFE

Ken Livingstone, the leader of the Greater London Council, who attempted to reduce London Underground fares, and was daubed 'Red Ken'.

The clock face of Big Ben in the Palace of Westminster with Westminster Bridge over the River Thames to the left.

Raymond Revue Bar

Striptease venues and 'erotic entertainment' on Brewer Street Soho.

MUSIC

ALBUMS RELEASED THIS YEAR

January	**Run DMC**	King Of Rock
February	**Phil Collins**	No Jacket Required
	Whitney Houston	Whitney Houston
	Tears For Fears	Songs From The Big Chair
	The Smiths	Meat Is Murder
March	**Luther Vandross**	The Night I Fell In Love
April	**Eurythmics**	Be Yourself Tonight
May	**Dire Straits**	Brothers In Arms
	New Order	Low-Life
	Prince	Around The World In A Day
June	**Prefab Sprout**	Steve McQueen
	Scritti Politti	Cupid & Pscyhe
	The Style Council	Our Favourite Shop
	REM	Fables Of The Reconstruction
	Talking Heads	Little Creatures
August	**The Cure**	The Head On The Door
	The Pogues	Rum, Sodomy & The Lash
September	**Kate Bush**	Hounds Of Love
	The Waterboys	This Is The Sea
October	**A Ha**	Hunting High And Low
	INXS	Listen Like Thieves
	Simple Minds	Once Upon A Time
	The Cult	Love
November	**Sade**	Promise
	The Jesus And Mary Chain	Pyschocandy
December	**Fine Young Cannibals**	Fine Young Cannibals

BIGGEST POP SONGS OF 1985

Jennifer Rush	The Power Of Love
Elaine Paige & Barbara Dixon	I Know Him So Well
Madonna	Into The Groove
Paul Hardcastle	19
Sister Sledge	Frankie
David Bowie + Mick Jagger	Dancing In The Street
Phyllis Nelson	Move Closer
Feargal Sharkey	A Good Heart
A Ha	Take On Me
King	Love & Pride
Foreigner	I Want To Know What Love Is
Phillip Bailey & Phil Collins	Easy Lover
Harold Faltermeyer	Axel F
Band Aid	Do They Know It's Christmas
UB40 + Chrissie Hynde	I Got You Babe
Madonna	Crazy For You
Whitney Houston	Saving All My Love For You
Ashford And Simpson	Solid
Dead Or Alive	You Sping Me Round (Like A Record)
Eurythmics	There Must Be An Angel (Playing With My Heart)
Wham!	I'm Your Man
Colonel Abrams	Trapped
Kool And The Gang	Cherish
Tears For Fears	Everybody Wants To Rule The World
Shakin' Stevens	Merry Christmas Everyone
The Crowd	You'll Never Walk Alone
Midge Ure	If I Was
Elton John	Nikita
Bruce Springsteen	Dancing In The Dark

Bonnie Tyler	Holding Out For A Hero
Marillion	Kayleigh
Wham!	Last Christmas/ Everything She Wants
Duran Duran	A View To A Kill
USA For Africa	We Are The World
Red Box	Lean On Me
Stevie Wonder	Part-Time Lover
Dire Straits	Money For Nothing
UB40	Don't Break My heart
Go West	We Close Our Eyes

LIVE AID

The Live Aid event was organised by Bob Geldof and Midge Ure in order to raise further funds for famine relief in Ethiopia. The even was held in July at Wembley Stadium in the UK and the John F Kennedy Stadium in Philadelphia. Queens live performance at the event has been voted the greatest live performance in the history or rock, opening with 'Bohemian Rhapsody'.

ELTON JOHN

This year, Elton released his 'Ice On Fire' album, which featured the big hit single 'Nikita' and also the song 'Wrap Her Up' featuring George Michael.

With Tina Turner & Terry Wogan

With his wife Renate

PRINCE

Following the enormous success of the 'Purple Rain' album the previous year, Prince released 'Around The World In A Day,' a very intense album but one that still birthed the incredible 'Raspberry Beret' single.

DUSTY SPRINGFIELD + KIM WILDE

SADE

Dusty Springfield, Janet Street Porter + Kim Wilde at the Hippodrome

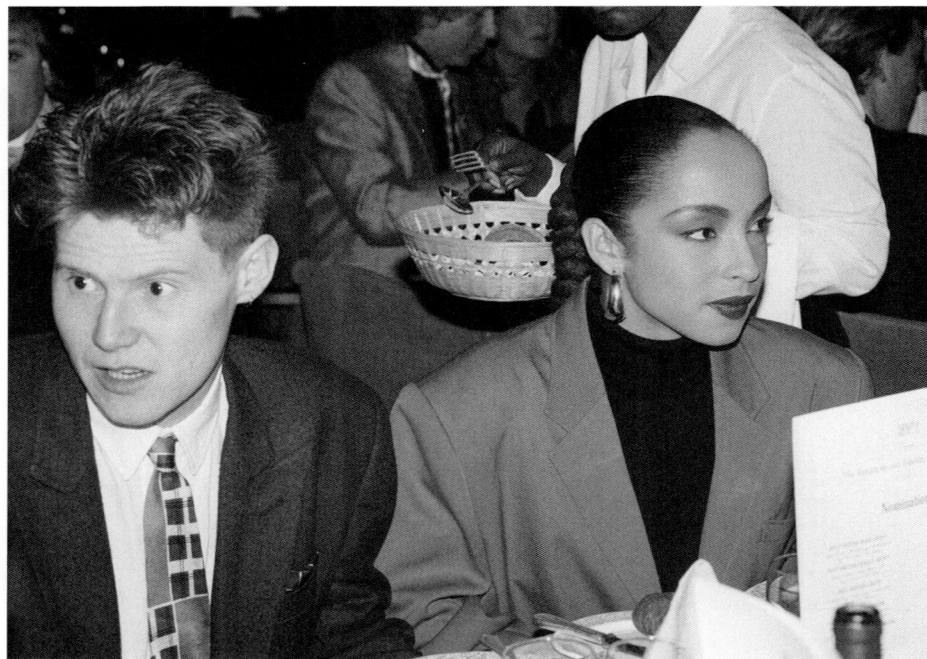

Singer and musician Sade, alongside her then boyfriend journalist and broadcaster Robert Elms at this years BPI Music Awards at the Grosvenor House Hotel.

PHIL COLLINS

Phil Collins released his album 'No Jacket Required' in February featuring the hits 'Sussudio' and 'Don't Lose My Number'. The album also featured Helen Terry, Peter Gabriel and Sting. The album reached number one in the UK for 5 consecutive weeks and for seven weeks in the US. It proved to be the second best selling album of 1985.

BANANARAMA

WHAM!

EURYTHMICS

The band released their 'Be Yourself Tonight' album this year which proved to be their most commercially successful and hit laden album. From 'Would I Lie To You', to 'There Must Be An Angel' and onto 'Sisters Are Doin It For Themselves' Rockers, feminist anthems, angelic vocals and guest features from the likes of Aretha Franklin and Stevie Wonder.

With Grace Jones + Dolph Lundgren

DURAN DURAN

The band had written the theme tune to the Bond film 'A View To A Kill'.

MADONNA

With Marilyn

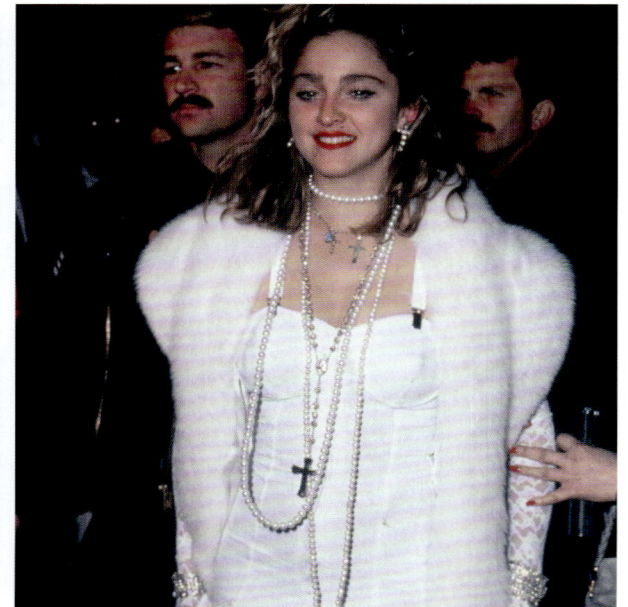

WHITNEY HOUSTON

Whitney pretty much changed the game this year with her self titled debut album. Huge R&B ballads, driven by the mighty powerful MTV. Songs like 'The Greatest Love Of All' and 'Saving All My Love For You' set the tone for the next decade.

JENNIFER RUSH

Her single 'The Power Of Love' was released in 1984 in West Germany without much success, but it slowly took hold and reached number one on the UK singles chart in October 1985 and became the biggest selling single of the year, and the ninth best selling single of the 1980's.

GRACE JONES

+ Duran Duran

STEVIE WONDER

Stevie released his 'In Square Circle' album which was driven by the hit 'Part Time Love'.

LIONEL RICHIE

With Loretta Lynn and Quincy Jones

BILLY JOEL

With Christine Brinkley

BONO/U2

BOB DYLAN

With David Bowie

BOY GEORGE + CULTURE CLUB

With Marilyn

With Freddie Mercury + Jane Seymour

RADIO & TV

EASTENDERS

The television soap opera Eastenders began its first broadcast in February of this year. It was set in the fictional borough of Walford in the East End of London. The programme always tackled many controversial and taboo subjects in British culture, and portrayed many aspects of life in the UK that had never previously been covered.

Pete Beale (Peter Dean)

Nick Cotton (John Altman)

Sharon Watts (Letitia Dean)

Other British tv debuts this year include 'Victoria Wood', 'Dempsey and Makepeace', 'Blind Date', 'The Cosby Show', 'Howards Way', and 'Children's BBC' is launched on BBC1 with Phillip Schofield presenting from 'The Broom Cupboard'.

Lorraine Chase

BBC weathermen

Kenny Everett

Radio 1 DJ's Janice Long, Steve Wright, Bruno Brookes & Simon Bates

Rula Lenska & Dennis Waterman

Gary Wilmot

Terry Wogan

David Jason

Felicity Kendal & Paul Eddington

'Doctor Who' Colin Baker

Spitting Image

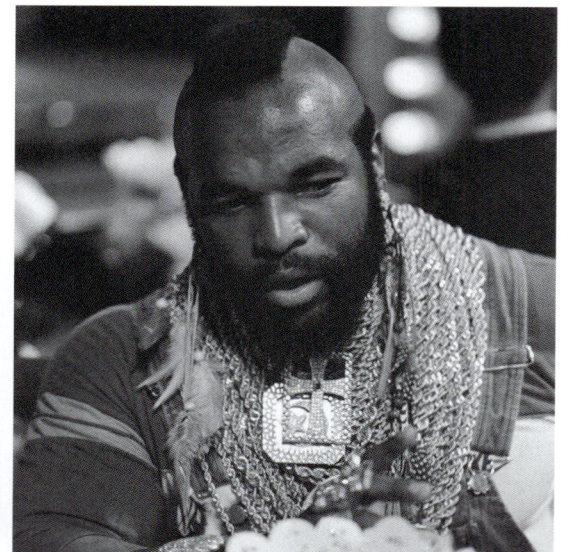
Mr T of the 'A Team'

STAGE & SCREEN

ROGER MOORE

'A View To A Kill' was this years James Bond film featuring Roger Moore as the fictional M16 agent. It was the third James Bond film to be directed by John Glen and the last to feature Lois Maxwell as Miss Moneypenny. The film was a major commercial success with the Duran Duran theme song performing very well in the charts, becoming the only Bond theme song to reach number one in the US and earning a Golden Globe nomination for Best Song. The film also features Grace Jones, Patrick McGee, Christopher Walken, Dolph Lundgren and Fiona Fullerton.

KELLY MCGILLIS

Kelly's breakout role occurred this year as an Amish mother in the film 'Witness' for which she received Golden Globe and BAFTA nominations. Just a year later she had the very high profile role of the flight instructor in the film 'Top Gun' starring Tom Cruise.

MICHELLE PFEIFFER

TOM SELLECK

Between 1980 and 1988 Tom enjoyed his break out role playing private investigator Thomas Magnum in the television series 'Magnum PI'. For this he received five Emmy nominations and he won Outstanding Lead Actor in a Drama series this year.

KIRK DOUGLAS

CLINT EASTWOOD

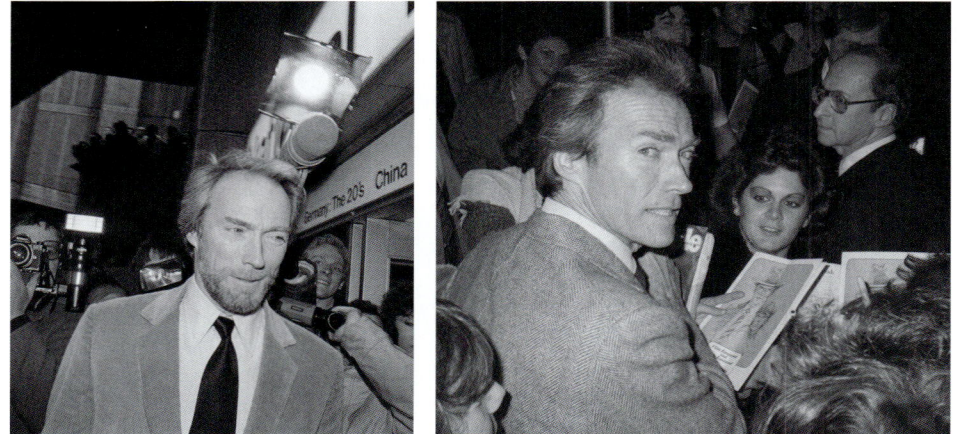

This year Eastwood featured in the 'Pale Rider' movie. Hailed as one of the best films of the year and the best western movie in quite some time.

ARNOLD SCHWARZENEGGER

MICHAEL J FOX

Fox hit the headlines this year playing Marty Mcfly in the 'Back to the Future' movie where he plays the teenager who is accidentally sent back in time to 1955. The film was an enormous commercial and critical success, spending eight consecutive weekends as the number one grossing movie in the US box office this year.

JENNY AGUTTER

TOM HANKS

MATT DILLON

IMAGE CREDITS

ALL IMAGES COURTESY OF GETTY IMAGES